Backyard Animals
Bears
Edited by Heather C. Hudak

Weigl Publishers Inc.

Published by Weigl Publishers Inc.
350 5th Avenue, Suite 3304, PMB 6G
New York, NY 10118-0069
Website: www.weigl.com

Library of Congress Cataloging-in-Publication Data available upon request.
Fax 1-866-44-WEIGL for the attention of the Publishing Records department.

ISBN 978-1-60596-000-5 (hard cover)
ISBN 978-1-60596-006-7 (soft cover)

Printed in the United States of America
1 2 3 4 5 6 7 8 9 0 12 11 10 09 08

Editor Heather C. Hudak
Design Terry Paulhus

All of the Internet URLs given in the book were valid at the time of publication.
However, due to the dynamic nature of the Internet, some addresses may have
changed, or sites may have ceased to exist since publication. While the author
and publisher regret any inconvenience this may cause readers, no responsibility
for any such changes can be accepted by either the author or the publisher.

Photo Credits

Weigl acknowledges Getty Images as its primary image supplier for this title.

Every reasonable effort has been made to trace ownership and to obtain permission
to reprint copyright material. The publishers would be pleased to have any errors
or omissions brought to their attention so that they may be corrected in
subsequent printings.

Contents

Meet the Bear

Bears are a type of **mammal**. They usually live by themselves and spend most of their time looking for food. Bears mostly eat plants, such as grasses and berries. They also eat fish, insects, and small animals.

Most bears are large animals with thick fur, round heads, and short tails. Their colors and sizes are different depending on the type of bear. Bears are known for their excellent sense of smell. They can be found all over the world. Most bears live in forests and caves.

Bears that live in parts of the world that have a winter season go into **hibernation**. When the weather gets cold, bears cuddle up in a cave or hollowed out tree for months, until spring comes. This way, they can stay warm and avoid the months when food is hard to find.

Fascinating Facts

The regular heartbeat of a bear is 40 to 50 beats per minute. During hibernation, it drops to 8 or 10.

Bears are one of the few animals that can stand up or walk on two feet.

All about Bears

There are many different types of bear, but only three **species** live in North America. These are brown bears, black bears, and polar bears.

Other types of bear include the giant panda bear, which lives in China, and the Sun bear, which lives in southeast Asia. Although there are differences between these species, they are all part of the bear family.

Most bears can live in different environments. They can change their diet, shelters, and habits to suit the places where they live.

Where Bears Live

Brown Bear
- Found in North America, Europe, and Asia

Polar Bear
- Lives in the cold Arctic regions

Asiatic Black Bear
- Found in Southern Asia

Spectacled Bear
- Lives in the forests of South America

Bear History

Bears come from an ancient animal called the *miacid*. This animal was small in size, had a snout, and lived 50 million years ago. Wolves, hyenas, and weasels also came from miacids.

About 38 million years ago, bearlike animals started to develop the features of bears today. They began to grow larger than other miacids, and their skulls became rounder. Ten million years ago, animals called *ursids* developed. Over time, they became the bears that are common today.

Fascinating Facts

Early ursids, such as the true cave bear, would compete with humans for habitat and food.

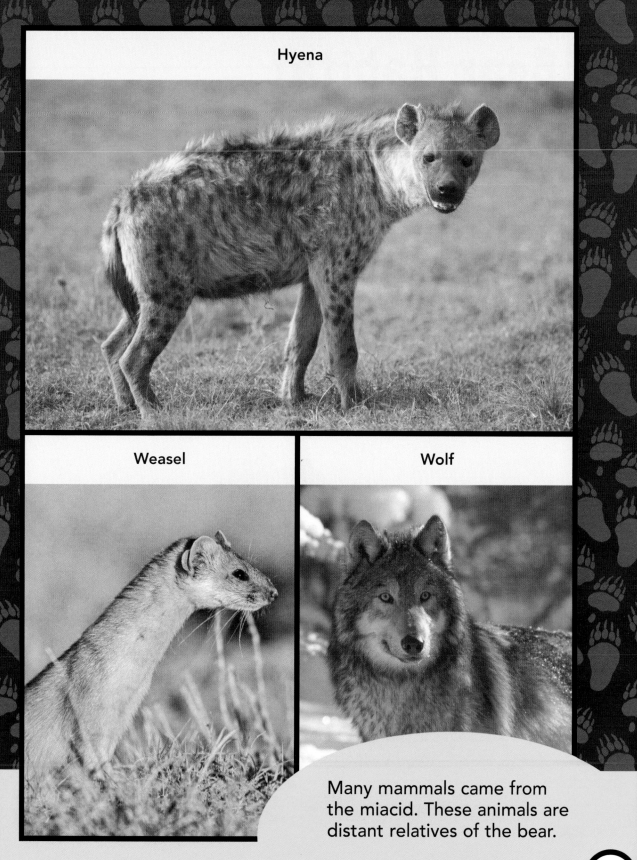

Hyena

Weasel

Wolf

Many mammals came from the miacid. These animals are distant relatives of the bear.

Bear Habitat

Bears can live in almost all environments. Some live in dense forests, while others live in cold, icy places. Most bears prefer to live away from humans. Some, such as the grizzly, live near campsites, where they hope to find leftover food.

Bears often live in forests that have water close by. Many bears live in **dens**. Dens can be inside caves or the hollow of a tree. Some bears can spend almost half of their lives in dens. They make their den with old leaves and plants.

Dens protect bears from bad weather and give them a place to hibernate in the winter.

The giant panda is one of the most distinct types of bear. It has very unique markings.

Bear Features

Bears have many features that help them run fast, find food, and hide from danger.

FUR
Bears have thick fur that helps them keep warm. The fur covers their entire body.

CLAWS
All bears have sharp claws that help them dig and rip through plants and trees. This is useful when bears need to turn, lift, or pull up objects to find food.

HEAD
Bears have large round skulls. They are smart animals with a fairly large brain.

SMELL
Most bears have an excellent sense of smell. This helps them find food easily. They use their nose to sniff out plants or animals that are nearby.

TEETH
Bears have strong teeth, with long **canines** to help them eat meat. The teeth are able to tear into tough meat easily.

What Do Bears Eat?

Bears are **omnivores**. This means that they eat both meat and plants. However, some types of bears have different diets. This diet depends on the place where the bear lives. If there are more plants, the bear is likely to eat less meat. The giant panda bear is a **herbivore**. Most of its diet is made up of bamboo.

If a bear lives where there is very little plant life, it will eat more meat. The polar bear is a **carnivore**. It eats mostly meat. Grizzly bears and black bears eat fish as a part of their diet. They have also been known to hunt large animals such as elk and bison.

The spectacled bear climbs trees to find food.

Fruit

Fish

Bamboo

Most bears eat a combination of foods to make up their diet. Some bears eat berries, while others eat fish or bamboo.

Bear Life Cycle

The life cycle of a bear depends on the type of bear. Grizzly bears mate between May and July. The male stays with the female for about one month. The female digs a den where she can hibernate for the winter.

Birth

A grizzly bear can have one to four cubs at the time. At birth, grizzly bear cubs cannot open their eyes. They are covered with very tiny hairs and have no teeth. At this stage, the cubs are helpless. Their mothers must care for them.

Early Months

The first few months of a cub's life are spent inside the den with its mother. The cub's eyes open after its first two or three weeks. The cub also starts to grow more hair. The mother bear feeds the cub her milk, which is full of fat and **protein**.

One to four cubs are born about four or five months later. The mother takes care of the cubs until they learn the skills they need to take care of themselves. Cubs stay with their mothers until they are about two years old.

First Year

As the weather outside gets warmer, the bears start to explore outside of the den. After six months, they can leave the den with their mother. At this stage, the cubs grow very fast. They learn skills, such as hunting, by watching their mother.

Encountering Bears

Bears live all over the world. They can be found in nature and in zoos. Some bears live in areas where there are more humans. They may be found near campgrounds in the woods.

Humans sometimes leave leftover food at campsites. Bears may come to the sites searching for food. It is very important to clean up so that bears are not encouraged to come to the sites. If a bear does show up at a site, it should not be approached. It is best to remain calm and leave the area slowly.

Some bears, such as the giant panda, are **endangered**. They are protected by laws that make harming them illegal.

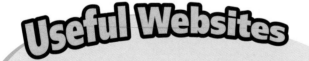

Useful Websites

Check out this site for more interesting information about bears.
www.bears.org

Trash and food should be stored safely to keep bears from coming to campsites.

Myths and Legends

There have been many stories about bears from all over the world. The ancient Greeks have a story about how the god Zeus turned a mother and son into bears and then placed them in the sky. Now, they appear as groups of stars known as Great Bear and Little Bear.

American Indians have many legends about bears. These stories talk about bears as animals that help heal sick people.

Great Bear can be seen in the night sky.

The Cherokee Bear Legend

The Ani-Tsa-gu-hi Cherokee lived near a forest. They worked very hard to find food. One family had a son who would spend all day in the forest. His parents worried about him. They asked him why he kept going into the forest. He told them that the forest was filled with food and life was easier there. The boy asked his family to come with him.

The boy's parents told the Ani-Tsa-gu-hi leaders the boy's story. After hearing it, they all decided to follow the boy into the forest.

Other groups rushed to convince them to change their minds, but the Ani-Tsa-gu-hi told the others that they had changed their name to the *Yonva*, which means "bears." The Yonva then went into the forest. As the other groups walked away, they looked back and saw a group of bears.

Frequently Asked Questions

Why do bears hibernate?

Answer: Many bears hibernate because they have fewer food sources in the winter. The weather is too cold for plants to grow. Bears spend these cold months in hibernation because it is a waste of their energy to try to find food in this environment.

Is the koala a bear?

Answer: Many people believe that the koala is a bear. Although it looks quite a bit like a bear, the koala is another type of animal called a marsupial.

How do bears communicate?

Answer: Bears can communicate with actions and sounds. The way a bear stands often shows the bear's mood. Bears make different sounds, such as growls. They also clack their teeth together.

Puzzler

See if you can answer these questions about bears.

1. What kind of animal is a bear?
2. How many cubs does a bear usually have at one time?
3. How many years does a grizzly bear cub stay with its mother?
4. What does the giant panda mostly eat?
5. When do bears hibernate?

Answers: 1. mammal 2. between one and four 3. two years 4. bamboo 5. in the cold winter months

Find Out More

There are many more interesting facts to learn about bears. Look for these books at your library so you can learn more.

Hunt, Joni Phelps, and Vicki Leon. *Band of Bears*. London Town Press, 2006.

Swanson, Diane. *Welcome to the World of Bears*. Whitecap Books, Ltd., 1997.

Words to Know

canines: sharp pointy teeth on either side of the mouth

carnivore: an animal that eats meat

dens: places where an animal lives in nature

endangered: to be at risk of disappearing

herbivore: an animal that eats plants

hibernation: a period during which an animal remains inactive

mammal: a warm-blooded animal that has a backbone and drinks milk from its mother

omnivores: animals that eat plants and other animals

protein: a substance found in all living things

species: a group of animals or plants that have many features in common

Index